Journey of  Renewal

THE ACCOUNTABILITY MOVEMENT
of The Salvation Army

First published 2016
Copyright © 2016 The General of The Salvation Army, inclusive of words, diagrams, artwork and images
ISBN 978-1-911149-09-5
e-book ISBN 978-1-911149-10-1

Design: James Gardner and Berni Georges

A catalogue record of this book is available from the British Library.

Bible references are from the *New International Version*, except where another translation is indicated in brackets.

References from *The Salvation Army Handbook of Doctrine* refer to the 2010 edition.

Song references are from *The Song Book of The Salvation Army* (2015).

Published by Salvation Books
The Salvation Army International Headquarters
101 Queen Victoria Street, London EC4V 4EH, United Kingdom

For more information please visit **www.salvationarmy.org/accountability**

Printed and bound in the UK by Page Bros Ltd

Contents

JOURNEY OF RENEWAL
Invitation from the General

As its international leader, I am convicted to call The Salvation Army to spiritual and missional renewal. In a world of shifting values, we must be people of spiritual vitality and integrity, faithful and dynamic in mission. We should want to be accountable for our actions and attitudes as we participate in God's mission to transform the world. We must be keen to learn from our successes, but also our failures. To address these vital concerns I am asking everyone linked to The Salvation Army to join an Accountability Movement.

What do we mean by 'accountability'? It is more than accounting for money. Accountability is a process which requires each and every person to be good stewards in every aspect of life. This includes being accountable to those who have authority over us, but also to people who support, benefit from or share in our work. Accountability enables greater personal and corporate integrity; more learning from successes and failures; respect for every person; more effective stewardship of all resources; the desire to report, explain and be answerable for consequences.

This is not new, but the voices calling for accountability are getting stronger and louder. Individuals, governments, corporations and organisations are being closely watched. For example, accountability has been placed at the heart of the new Sustainable Development Goals adopted by all 193 member states of the United Nations in September 2015. We will all be called to account for our actions in this world, and the next.

We must not rest on a reputation built by the generations of courageous, dedicated Salvationists who have gone before us. We have been given a great foundation over the past 150 years but we now need to move forward. Salvationists and those who work with us are right to expect greater accountability, transparency and good stewardship of all our resources. People want to know where we are going – now. It is not enough to dwell on past achievements. People simply ask: 'Show me what difference you are making – today!'

In some places in the world, past failings are catching up with us. Handling this is not easy. It is very painful and we must do everything possible to not make the same mistakes in the future. We need to learn afresh the gospel values of integrity, servanthood and transparency. Many parts of the Army are already bearing fruit because they have taken, and continue on, a journey of renewal. They have become accountable for the future, both to God and each other. When we live out our holiness, in the power of the Holy Spirit and the love of Christ, the difference is clear for all to see. In these places, we are making excellent progress in God's great mission of 'saving souls, growing saints and serving suffering humanity'.

I encourage every person linked to The Salvation Army to read this book and use the Mission Accountability Framework. I am praying that the Accountability Movement will result in The Salvation Army experiencing a fresh momentum in mission and holy living. I pray we will all be more like Jesus in every dimension of life.

May God help us all make this a reality in The Salvation Army in every place.

General André Cox
June 2016

 FOR REFLECTION

1. Why is accountability becoming an increasingly important issue across the world?

2. Why do you think the General is calling everyone linked to The Salvation Army to be more accountable through a journey of renewal?

3. How do you think this invitation from the General can be made relevant, even urgent, where you are – in your corps, centre, team, division, territory or other expression of The Salvation Army?

4. How is accountability – as defined by the General – relevant in your life?

 NOTES

 NOTES

How to Use
This Book

Introduction

Introduction:
How to use this book

This book provides a flexible, simple resource to strengthen a culture of accountability in all parts of The Salvation Army. It will help facilitate greater health and dynamism of the Army's spiritual life and mission around the world. It introduces the key elements of the Accountability Movement and will help us get going on this important journey. It will be translated into the main languages spoken by Salvationists around the world.

The book's main message is that a strong, vibrant accountability movement in The Salvation Army goes hand in hand with a deep experience of spiritual and missional renewal. You cannot have one without the other. It requires us to have the vision and energy to be accountable as well as being committed and intentional on our journey through life with God.

This is true on a personal level and a corporate level. Each of us must take stock personally, but so must whole corps, centres, teams, leadership teams, divisions and territories. All of us, in every place, can be responsible for the future of The Salvation Army, spiritually and missionally. We are reminded of this at various points throughout this book.

Who should read this book and why?

Journey of Renewal aims to help everyone connected with The Salvation Army – adherents, junior and senior soldiers, volunteers, employees, friends, donors, advisers, officers, corporate and other partners – to explore what God wants of us and have the ability to explain where we are going, how we will get there and the difference we are making. When we do that we are being accountable. The Salvation Army will be an even more faithful member of the Body of Christ serving in the world and people will be inspired and influenced by the gospel.

Brief summary

Journey of Renewal has been written for use in all parts of the world and in all contexts. The General's 'Invitation' and chapter 1's 'True Story' of renewal and accountability are important starting points. They get us thinking more intentionally about the health of our spiritual life and mission right where we are. The questions at the end of the 'Invitation' and the 'True Story' help us explore how renewal and accountability can be a vital journey for us all. Flashbacks to the 'True Story' later in the book help illustrate key accountability concepts as they are unpacked.

In chapter 2, the book provides some historical insight into the Army being accountable for its ongoing life and mission. But the real challenge of this chapter is about how we do this in the very different world of the 21st century. The chapter and the reflection questions at the end help us see and respond to this critical difference.

Mission Accountability Framework

In chapters 3 to 9, *Journey of Renewal* introduces and unpacks the Mission Accountability Framework (MAF), the primary tool of the Accountability Movement. The six dimensions of the MAF provide a structure for an accountability review. We can use it as individuals to check we are being faithful and effective on the journey. We can also use the MAF to structure a review with a mentor or friend. It can also be used by teams or groups of people.

The power of the MAF to help us is in its questions. The questions are challenging:

- How are my relationships with people?

- What is my purpose on the journey under review? What am I trying to achieve?

- Do I have a plan? Is it helpful? Does it need to be updated?

- What outcomes am I achieving on the journey?

- Am I using all available procedures and systems to help me on my journey?

- Most importantly, how are my energy levels – physically, emotionally, spiritually? Am I being renewed day by day?

The MAF does not give the answers; it asks questions. The answers will vary around the world, but these are important questions for everyone.

Flashbacks to the 'True Story' in chapter 1 actually expand on the story and will inspire readers about how the accountability concepts discussed in each dimension can become a reality at the front line of mission.

The Bible readings and songs included with each dimension can be used by individuals and groups to reflect on their journey during devotions and retreats. Other spiritual and devotional helps can be included as necessary. Leaders, facilitators and mission practitioners are encouraged to think creatively about the use of available resources.

The MAF can be used by a group of people to review a programme or activity. The Salvation Army's official accountability processes can use the MAF to structure territorial, divisional, corps and centre reviews, audits and personnel reviews. The MAF can be used to check that existing reviews cover all six key dimensions and ask the right questions.

Journey of Renewal also encourages the use of the Faith-Based Facilitation process (see chapter 10) to help answer the questions in each dimension of the MAF. For example, it is important to have a good process in developing a plan. The issues arising from the MAF questions must be described and analysed; the issues must be reflected upon in the light of the Bible and the experience of the Army and the wider Church. The Holy Spirit must be listened to in our planning and at every stage on our journey of renewal.

As the psalmist sang thousands of years ago:

'Unless the LORD builds the house, the builders labour in vain.

Unless the LORD watches over the city, the guards stand watch in vain.'

Psalm 127:1

As the Accountability Movement spreads around the world, resources and lessons learnt will be posted on the Web.

Visit **www.salvationarmy.org/accountability**

You can also go to **www.facebook.com/salvationarmyam** and join the Facebook page 'The Salvation Army's Accountability Movement' for the latest news.

JOURNEY OF RENEWAL
A True Story

Chapter 1

1

JOURNEY OF RENEWAL
A True Story

ieutenants Bram and Eva* were in the second year of their first appointment as corps officers, leading the mission of The Salvation Army in a town called Richmond*. The town's population was about 20,000 and many more people lived in villages nearby.

Bram and Eva were passionate new lieutenants with a big vision. Their lives, and the lives of their children, had been turned around when they met Jesus Christ and put everything into God's hands. They had experienced a transformation from darkness to light, from material pursuits to spiritual depth, from a lacklustre life to one of great hope and purpose. They envisaged such transformation for the people of Richmond.

As soon as they arrived it was clear that Richmond Corps was not ready for such a monumental vision. Work needed to be done on preparing the hearts and minds of the corps people to engage in dynamic Christian mission. Despite having good relationships with the community, its local government and leading citizens for more than 100 years, the average attendance at worship meetings had never grown beyond 50. Why was that, they wondered?

In fact, the lieutenants could not understand why questions of mission impact and stewardship of resources had not been seriously addressed. Why did people not see the importance of being accountable to God for their part in his mission? The lieutenants did not let it bother them too much.

They started by working intentionally on relationships. They built relationships with the corps people, including holding a retreat to consider what the people wanted to see their corps become and how that might happen. They also considered their community, its distinct characteristics and what it would take to see people's lives transformed by Jesus. The lieutenants also organised a training course on what team leadership involved, both as individuals and as a group. Regular training and learning together were key to the change process that gradually began to take root.

The new leadership group started taking ownership of the corps' future, speaking to others about it, and a new vision took shape and gained momentum. Lieutenants Bram and Eva preached from the Word of God about the purpose of the corps, focusing on the example of Jesus who, they would often say, helps us live, breathe and speak the values of the Kingdom of God in every part of life. Corps people who had lived without change for many years, seeing officers come and go, began to think something different might be possible.

The corps hall was in a poor condition. It was in urgent need of either renovation or replacement. Again, the lieutenants wondered why the property had been allowed to deteriorate. Did no one care? But something wonderful happened soon after they discussed their concerns with the corps people. A property became available on the other side of town in an area with many new houses, and the Army bought it. The sale of the old corps hall in Richmond's central business district, plus local fundraising and some support from territorial headquarters (THQ), helped fund the purchase. There were some complaints about moving but most of the people were excited. Something different was not only possible but was happening. The new corps building was bigger with more potential to serve the community.

By the start of the lieutenants' second year, the corps had moved into its new home, new people had started coming to Sunday meetings and other corps activities began to flourish. People in the community started to notice something was happening at The Salvation Army. Things had progressed very fast, almost like a miracle had occurred.

However, Lieutenant Bram felt something was missing. He felt the change was still fragile and began seeking God like he had never done before. Bram was concerned there was little evidence of people's lives being transformed by Jesus. It was great to have a new building, but what would it take to see the building overflowing with people finding new life and hope in Christ? He had experienced new life from Jesus and he desperately wanted the same for others.

A few weeks later, Lieutenant Bram attended a conference. One speaker spoke right into Bram's heart. 'It was like the sword of the Spirit piercing my heart and mind,' Bram said. Zechariah 4:6 became a very important verse: '"Not by might, nor by power, but by my Spirit," says the LORD Almighty.' And also Ephesians 6:10-18, ending with the powerful injunction: 'And pray in the Spirit on all occasions with all kinds of prayers and requests.'

Suddenly, it dawned on Lieutenant Bram: the mission of The Salvation Army is a spiritual mission that requires spiritual power, energy and foresight to drive it. Things were out of balance, he thought. Too much focus on doing the work and nowhere near enough prayer and knowing the person and power of the Holy Spirit to fuel all the energy. The corps people were in love with the Army and its history – but they did not have enough love for God. Lieutenant Bram realised his people needed to learn to love prayer, where the Holy Spirit prepares our spirit for dynamic mission.

Bram knew such prayer needed to include 'warfare' prayer, where a church identifies and prays powerfully against strongholds that blind people to their need for God. He realised Richmond Corps, and probably many other corps he had attended in the past, were running on half-empty. No one had stopped, it seemed to him, to do a spiritual check-up. No one had asked why people lacked real passion for God.

When he returned to the corps from the conference it was like Bram was on fire, and the fire started spreading. He preached on the power of prayer in relation to mission, including warfare prayer, for 10 straight weeks. Lieutenant Eva caught the fire too and began encouraging the women of the corps to go deeper with God. Prayer groups and Bible study groups began popping up all over the town, including early in the morning. A new excitement about knowing Jesus gripped the corps and the corps people couldn't keep it to themselves.

People started coming to Jesus in significant numbers and the corps grew rapidly during the next two years. The youth group came alive and young people from the high schools starting showing up at the corps and finding new life and hope in Jesus. Some of the newcomers were musicians and the worship life of the corps was transformed. Tithes and offerings increased, not only because of the increase in numbers, but also because people simply wanted to give more. Testimonies about being transformed in Jesus were heard often.

Mission Accountability – A Journey of Renewal

The story of the change at Richmond Corps is a true story. It is an encouraging story and we share it with you because, in these challenging days of the 21st century, God is longing for all parts of The Salvation Army to go on a journey of spiritual and mission renewal. This is at the heart of the Accountability Movement. It is not firstly about money, or systems, or regulations – it is about spiritual and mission renewal.

No part of The Salvation Army is perfect. We can all be more effective for God if we are willing to go on a journey of renewal. This book, and the Accountability Movement it introduces, aims to create healthy and sustainable mission in every part of The Salvation Army, and in every person's life – mission that impacts our world with the love and power of God in Christ. Journey of Renewal introduces a Mission Accountability Framework through which we can be accountable for the impact of our mission in an ongoing way. It helps us to ask the right questions and to feel safe in doing so.

In the chapters of *Journey of Renewal* that describe the Mission Accountability Framework there will be flashbacks to the story of Richmond Corps, showing clearly how renewal and accountability in mission are intrinsically linked and vital to the life of The Salvation Army in every place.

* Not real names or places

 FOR REFLECTION

1. What part of this true story did you find most interesting? Have you experienced something similar when God's Spirit renews his people?

2. At Richmond Corps there were many outcomes from the officers and leadership team becoming more accountable for the health of the corps. What were some of these outcomes? How do these relate to The Salvation Army where you are, whether a corps, centre, team, division, territory or other expression of Salvation Army work?

3. Which attitudes and behaviours changed in this story? What changes might be needed where you are?

 NOTES

NOTES

JOURNEY OF RENEWAL
Building an Accountability Movement

Chapter 2

JOURNEY OF RENEWAL
Building an Accountability Movement

2015 MARKED 150 YEARS since The Salvation Army began its work as The Christian Mission in the East End of London. Empowered by the Holy Spirit, a people's movement swept across England, Scotland, Wales and Ireland. Women, men, girls and boys joined the Army in their thousands. Lives were changed. Communities were transformed. The Salvation Army movement soon spread around the world. The first Salvationists lived, breathed and preached a message of boundless salvation for all. They were deeply committed and made incredible sacrifices to share the gospel.

The Salvation Army has kept marching along. As this table shows, the expansion of the Army in terms of countries has been consistent – and has accelerated since 1985.

International spread of the Army							
Year	Countries	Year	Countries	Year	Countries	Year	Countries
1865	1	1905	41	1945	70	1985	89
1870	1	1910	46	1950	71	1990	96
1875	1	1915	49	1955	71	1995	103
1880	4	1920	54	1960	73	2000	107
1885	17	1925	61	1965	75	2005	111
1890	26	1930	65	1970	78	2010	121
1895	32	1935	70	1975	83	2015	127
1900	35	1940	74	1980	85		

The number of people becoming Salvation Army soldiers also continues to increase.

Soldier numbers through the years					
Year	Soldiers	Year	Soldiers	Year	Soldiers
1900	193,092	1940	563,991*	1980	661,526
1905	217,738	1945	580,912*	1985	735,063
1910	231,382	1950	505,532	1990	776,684
1915	256,214	1955	532,752	1995	834,379
1920	334,660*	1960	560,576	2000	1,019,137
1925	442,427*	1965	580,047	2005	1,045,253
1930	487,815*	1970	595,191	2010	1,123,048
1935	537,245*	1975	634,395	2013	1,174,238

However, there is no room for complacency. The challenge for The Salvation Army as we move into the next 150 years is always to be what God wants us to be.

Everyone can be involved in the Accountability Movement

Journey of Renewal aims to help people – in every part of The Salvation Army and at every level – to be more accountable in all aspects of life.

Wherever there is a quality team (whether in a Salvation Army school, hospital, corps, centre, division or territory) there is much Kingdom fruit. That does not mean there are no problems. Often there are many serious challenges, such as shortages of money, inadequate buildings and inefficient management systems. Sadly, we must recognise that relationships inside The Salvation Army can be strained and damaged. We can improve. Despite the challenges, people seeking spiritual and mission renewal prioritise building deeper relationships with God, each other and the world around us. God blesses our work when we are accountable and faithful.

The early Salvation Army was good at developing leaders at every level. Every soldier had a responsibility. The strength of the corps was not the corps officer – they were often moved twice a year. Corps leadership depended on the quality of the local officers who were deeply committed and involved in leading their corps. Teenagers opened new corps and preached many times a week. People in their thirties and forties were appointed to lead growing territories. Women were given leadership opportunities in opposition to the culture of the time. Older people were not left out. There was a job for everyone at The Salvation Army.

Such a spirit of innovation and opportunity is needed today

The Salvation Army must always strive to do better. We need to live and work much more effectively, efficiently and faithfully for God. To do this we need a framework to help people working in The Salvation Army around the world be more effective, efficient and faithful builders of God's Kingdom. This book is a tool to help people track progress on their journey. While headquarters, regulators, corporate partners and donors are also concerned about accountability, it should be everyone's personal desire and priority to be accountable.

Why do we need an Accountability Movement?

A Salvation Army leader in India, Colonel Thumati Vijayakumar, who was promoted to Glory in February 2016, defined accountability as simply 'the ability to give an account'. This is a helpful, clear definition. To encourage others to live the life of boundless salvation that God desires for everyone, we need the ability to explain where we are going, how we will get there and the difference we are making.

Unfortunately, the word 'accountability' makes some people defensive or nervous. Many have negative experiences of accountability. It has been used to control or punish people. That is not what is envisioned for The Salvation Army's Accountability Movement. Accountability must be a positive resource on our Christian pilgrimage – we all need to be able to account for our actions and attitudes to God, each other and the world around us.

We are called to serve the present age. Around the world people linked to The Salvation Army are under close scrutiny – both corporately and individually. We urgently need resources to help people – in all parts of the Army – increase our ability to give an account.

Here are a few reasons to explain why accountability is important:

1. **We are accountable to God.** We are ultimately accountable to God – our creator – as stewards of his creation. Our 11th Doctrine teaches us that we will need to give an account when we come face-to-face with God, but that is not the only time we must be accountable. We require accountability each and every day if we are to reflect the mind and nature of Christ and live a holy life.

2. We are accountable to each other. This principle can often be overlooked in a hierarchical organisation. It is tempting for Christian leaders to think they are only accountable to God. The history of the Church is full of leaders who stopped listening to people. While The Salvation Army is not democratic, neither should it be autocratic. Rather, we believe God wants servant leaders at all levels of The Salvation Army.

As servant leaders, we need to strengthen our systems and practices so that we are accountable to each other. This renewed emphasis on accountability should result in people in every ministry of the Army taking personal responsibility for their part of the vineyard. The Salvation Army must be a movement of people of all ages, all occupations, from all nations, who are called and empowered 'to preach the gospel of Jesus Christ and to meet human needs in his name without discrimination', as stated in The Salvation Army's international mission statement.

3. We are accountable for the way we live every moment of every day. This is a huge concept with significant implications. We are accountable for how we handle all the resources given to us, including our care of the Earth. We must be good stewards in all things. This is central to our understanding of holiness.

There is no greater responsibility than how we treat other people. At times in the past we have not always treated people – both children and adults – as God expects. There have been times when both individuals in The Salvation Army and The Salvation Army as a whole have disregarded accountability or not exercised it appropriately when it comes to people and human vulnerability. People, who are made in the image of God, should never be treated as a tool to be used or a commodity to be bought. No one should ever be abused. Everyone – children and adults – must be valued as unique members of humanity. We will be held to account for the way we treat every person.

4. We are accountable for learning and improving. As we journey through life we need to have tools to track our progress and learn from our successes and failures. We need to measure our progress and understand the difference we are making so we can learn and improve. Too often measurement is seen as something that has to be done for headquarters, donors or the government. Our first priority in measurement should be for self-assessment – we want to know what difference we are making so we can learn and improve.

5. We need processes and systems that are fit for our God-given purpose. The Salvation Army works in 127 countries with millions of people serving in our ranks and impacted by our work. We require systems – governance, management, measurement, finance, property, personnel, safeguarding – to achieve our mission. We already have many existing systems, but these must be regularly reviewed to ensure they are fit for God's purpose.

Accountability – a reflection on Ephesians 4

Accountability is an often used word and is easily misunderstood, but it is nothing new for Christians. The church at Ephesus faced challenges and the advice given to them is still relevant for The Salvation Army today: 'Speaking the truth in love, we will grow to become in every respect the mature body of him who is the head, that is, Christ' (Ephesians 4:15). This verse captures the key element of the culture of accountability that God desires: we will be accountable when we can 'speak the truth in love' to each other. The reason accountability is so important is because it results in us growing 'to become in every respect the mature body of … Christ'.

We are not mature in Christ when we are not accountable to each other. When we do not speak or hear the truth in love we are immature. This is why the Accountability Movement is so important – it will increase our ability to speak and hear the truth in a spirit of love so that every part of The Salvation Army grows into the mature Body of Christ.

There is truth to be spoken. We must not ignore our failings. We must not sweep problems under the carpet and pretend all is well. We must be brave and face issues. Of course, not everything is wrong in the Army. There are many, many good examples of faithful people being fruitful and transforming lives right where they are. We need to be inspired by their example and learn from them.

'Becoming in every respect the mature body' requires a complete review of all aspects of Salvation Army life. Therefore, part of the Accountability Movement is a review of Salvation Army governance structures. This will include the way we measure the impact of our work, as well as our finance systems and policies, and how we better safeguard adults and children. It has to be a complete, integrated initiative. Obviously this will take time and require a substantial, sustained effort. Not everything can be done at once, but the overall purpose has to be clear to everyone – we want to be in every respect the mature body of Christ so that we can serve God and God's world.

Not a new idea

God has been calling people to account since Adam and Eve started eating forbidden fruit! The Bible is full of people being held to account for the way they lived. The Early Church made accountability a priority (see Acts 2:42-47). The early Salvation Army made accountability a priority. General William Booth adapted proven practices of the 1870s to develop measurement systems, accountability systems and regulations for his new Salvation Army. We must build on this rich heritage and use the best methods available in the 21st century to help us be more effective, efficient and faithful.

From the earliest days, there were concerns when Salvation Army ministry focused on 'serving' people without 'solving' the underlying issue. General Booth was alert to the risk of creating dependency. This is a priority in building an international Accountability Movement. We must reduce dependency and empower people to take greater responsibility for their attitudes and actions.

However, The Salvation Army knows that human efforts to address problems can be only one part of the solution. We believe people need boundless salvation – in all its dimensions – and that is only possible by God's grace. The Salvation Army was founded by the Booths with an integrated understanding of salvation: 'save souls, grow saints and serve suffering humanity,' as General John Gowans said. This is our integrated, holistic mission. The MAF (see chapters 3 to 9) helps people explore what boundless salvation could look like in their lives and for their communities. It will help people plan and track progress towards life in all its fullness – as offered by Jesus (John 10:10).

How did the Accountability Movement develop?

Two initiatives to strengthen measurement and accountability in The Salvation Army were started in 2013. People from all around The Salvation Army were involved. In July 2013, the Chief of the Staff appointed the One Army Accountability Review Group at International Headquarters (IHQ). The group began by writing to every territory, command and region to seek opinions on existing Salvation Army accountability systems and 93 per cent responded. Two main areas of concern were identified:

1. A lack of accountability in our relationships with each other.
2. The ineffectiveness and inefficiency of some accountability systems.

The review group addressed the issues raised and reported to the International Conference of Leaders (ICL) in Singapore in July 2014. The ICL endorsed the progress made and recommended that a group of senior leaders take it further.

At the same time, the One Army Impact Initiative started work, in collaboration with The Bridgespan Group, with the aim of strengthening measurement and learning across The Salvation Army. More than 600 Salvation Army personnel responded to an electronic survey asking about existing measurement systems and the use of statistics. The survey found that:

- 83 per cent of respondents are clear on the impact they seek through The Salvation Army – primarily, spiritual growth in people and communities;

- Statistics in The Salvation Army are mainly used for reporting – not for learning;

- Many people are concerned that statistics are not accurate and do not reflect the true impact of the work. People believe that statistics are not reported honestly because of a fear of showing 'bad' results;

- Personal stories are one of the best methods to explain the difference The Salvation Army is making.

The impact measurement work is now part of the Accountability Movement. It includes people from all five Salvation Army zones across the world, who are developing resources to help strengthen measurement and learning in the Army globally. These will be piloted and then rolled out over a number of years.

FOR REFLECTION

1. Accountability is 'the ability to give an account'. What has helped you to be accountable in your journey through life to this point in time?

2. Read Ephesians chapter 4 – what are the characteristics of a mature Christian?

3. The younger generations of today have grown up in a vastly different context to that of many older Salvationists. It is vital for the future of The Salvation Army that we become accountable to reach and engage people who see the world very differently to us. How can we learn to see through their eyes, walk in their shoes and reach their hearts?

 NOTES

 NOTES

The Mission
Accountability
Framework

Chapter 3

The Mission Accountability Framework

To ensure that the 'One Army with One Mission and One Message' vision is more than a slogan, we need a framework to help us all be accountable to God and each other. 'Being on a journey' is the idea at the heart of The Salvation Army's Accountability Movement. This is not a new idea. We already use many 'journey' words in our Christian lives. For example: pilgrimage, mission, march, race, campaign, quest, fight, movement and dance.

Everyone in The Salvation Army can use the Mission Accountability Framework (MAF) – from the youngest junior soldier to the General; from the professional social worker to the trombone player in the band. This is an ambitious statement. Can we have one MAF that is as relevant to Salvationists in the highlands of Papua New Guinea as for Salvationists in The Netherlands? We think this is possible if we answer a common set of questions. Of course, the answers to the questions will vary depending on the local context.

Answering the questions will not be easy, but using a reflective process such as Faith-Based Facilitation (FBF) will help. See chapter 10 of this book for a description of the FBF process and how to use it.

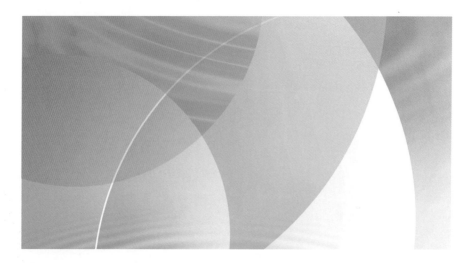

Mission Accountability Framework

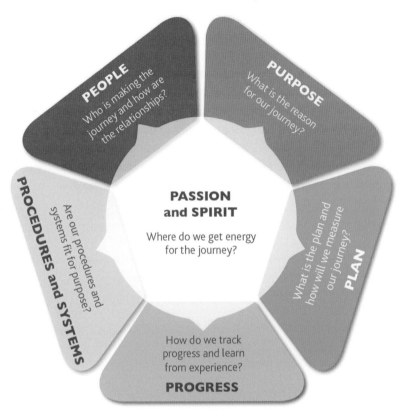

The key questions for accountability are explored in six dimensions in the MAF:

1. People.

2. Passion and Spirit.

3. Purpose.

4. Plan.

5. Progress.

6. Procedures and Systems.

In chapters 4 to 9 of this book, each dimension is briefly explained. Then chapter 10 gives guidance about how to get the most out of the MAF using the FBF process. Please remember, the MAF is designed to ask questions – it does not give the answers. You must answer the questions provided in your context. The answers will vary around the world.

To help guide the discussion, flashbacks to the 'True Story' in chapter 1 and some Bible verses and songs from the Song Book of The Salvation Army are included with each dimension. The MAF offers a structure for accountability discussions, but the pages of the Bible and the Song Book are full of guidance on how to live as God intends.

It is recommended to start every accountability discussion with the 'people' question: Who is making the journey and how are the relationships?

 NOTES

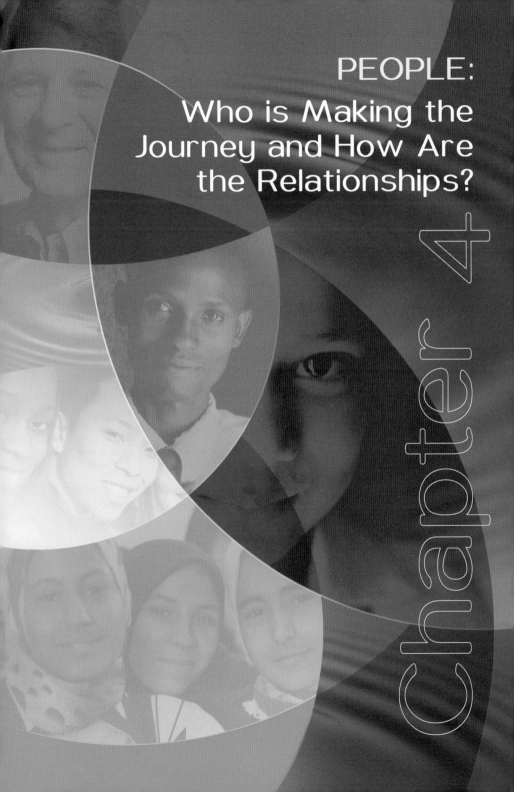

PEOPLE:
Who is Making the Journey and How Are the Relationships?

Chapter 4

PEOPLE:
Who is Making the Journey and How Are the Relationships?

Accountability discussions should start with questions about people. Too often the focus is on money, programmes, budgets or regulations. We believe people are made in God's image. God's priority is people and it must also be ours. Everyone working and serving in The Salvation Army needs to be helped to understand the importance of valuing people and building deeper relationships. In life, people can be treated as a tool to be used or a commodity to be bought. Many are treated badly by those in authority who abuse their power. We must be held to account for the way we treat people. The MAF emphasises the importance of tracking the quality of our relationships.

Problems arise when people are not sure who is responsible and what they are accountable for. Therefore, the first question to be answered is: 'Who is making the journey and how are the relationships?'

Being held to account for the character of our relationships is not easy. How are your relationships? Not just in the family or at work but also at the corps; with your neighbours? As Christians we are accountable for the character of our relationships. To what extent are our relationships holy and characterised by love, trust, hope, integrity, justice, humility and forgiveness? How are we encouraging these characteristics in our communities? Can we 'speak the truth in love' to each other?

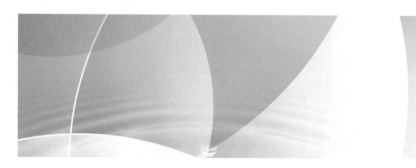

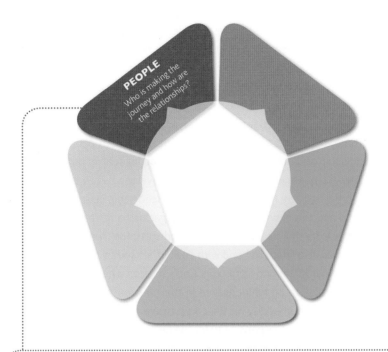

PEOPLE
Who is making the journey and how are the relationships?

QUESTIONS

- Who is making the journey and how are the relationships?
- To what extent are our relationships holy and characterised by love, trust, hope, integrity, justice, humility and forgiveness?
- How do we encourage these characteristics in our communities?
- Can we 'speak the truth in love' to each other?

FLASHBACK: **The True Story – PEOPLE**

Perhaps the most critical element of the journey of renewal undertaken by Richmond Corps, as outlined in chapter 1, was that it started with people. Upon arrival, Lieutenants Bram and Eva intentionally set out to both know the people of Richmond Corps and inspire them to take the journey.

Within weeks they had personally visited many people in their homes or met them at a local café. This included whole families, couples and individuals; older members of the corps living in retirement accommodation were not left out. They discovered hurts from the past that had never properly healed, hurts caused when people in the corps had not treated each other with respect and with the love of God. They talked with people about their life with God, their involvement in mission, their hopes for the corps, their personal struggles and fears. They prayed with them.

During this time, the lieutenants also identified leaders, both people already in positions of leadership and others who they thought had leadership potential – who had natural leadership qualities that had never been developed. They began working with this group, bringing them together for a series of leadership classes.

The lieutenants and the new leadership group organised a retreat for the whole corps, creating space for the seeds of spiritual and missional renewal to grow in people's hearts. It was also space to bond with each other and to be refreshed in the idea that the mission of Richmond Corps was God's mission. They were called, both individually and together, to be fully engaged in that mission as the people of God and began to see that accountability for the corps' future did not rest on the officers alone. They also began to take responsibility for the health of their own relationships, in some cases acknowledging past grievances and hurts, apologising to one another, and seeking God at the centre of their relationships.

Bible readings and songs | PEOPLE

The value of people to God

Genesis 1:27: 'So God created humankind in his image, in the image of God he created them' (*New Revised Standard Version – NRSV*).

Psalm 8:3-6: 'When I look at your heavens, the work of your fingers, the moon and the stars that you have established; what are human beings that you are mindful of them, mortals that you care for them? Yet you have made them a little lower than God, and crowned them with glory and honour. You have given them dominion over the works of your hands; you have put all things under their feet' (*NRSV*).

The character of our relationships

Matthew 22:36-40: '"Teacher, which is the greatest commandment in the Law?" Jesus replied: "Love the Lord your God with all your heart and with all your soul and with all your mind." This is the first and greatest commandment. And the second is like it: "Love your neighbour as yourself." All the Law and the Prophets hang on these two commandments.'

Galatians 5:22-23: 'The fruit of the Spirit is love, joy, peace, patience, kindness, generosity, faithfulness, gentleness, and self-control' (*NRSV*).

Ephesians 4:15-16: 'Speaking the truth in love, we must grow up in every way into him who is the head, into Christ, from whom the whole body, joined and knit together by every ligament ... as each part is working properly, promotes the body's growth in building itself up in love' (*NRSV*).

> You have given me a place to be,
> Made in the likeness of God,
> Only angels are ahead of me,
> Made in the likeness of God.
>
> *Crowned with glory and honour,*
> *Made in the likeness of God,*
> *Given dominion in all the earth,*
> *Made in the likeness of God.*
>
> **Joy Webb** *SASB* 381

See also:

SASB 139: 'He came to give us life in all its fullness'
SASB 418: 'Every day they pass me by (People need the Lord)'
SASB 813: 'For I'm building a people of power'
SASB 1010: 'Peace in our time, O Lord, to all the peoples – peace!'

NOTES

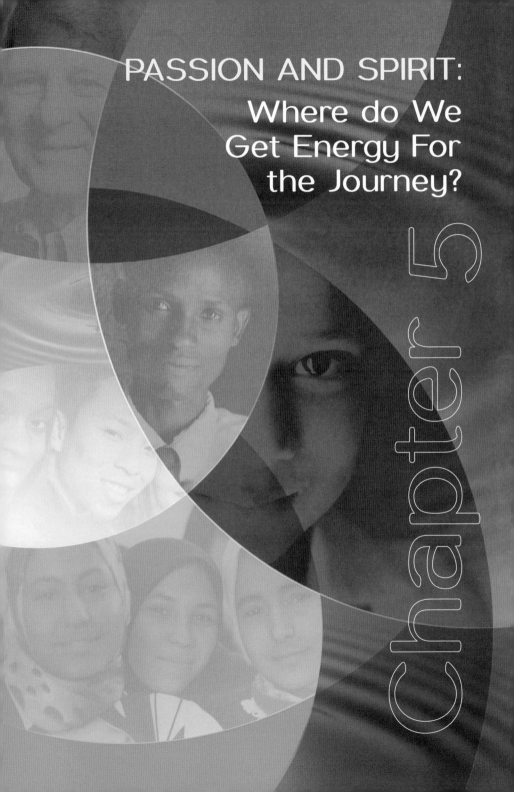

PASSION AND SPIRIT:
Where do We Get Energy For the Journey?

Chapter 5

PASSION AND SPIRIT:
Where do We Get Energy For the Journey?

At the centre of the MAF is passion and spirit. At the heart of our journey should always be our faith in the Lord Jesus Christ and the power of the Holy Spirit. Our passion and energy must come from our faith in God – Father, Son and Spirit.

When he was on Earth, Jesus spoke about the difficulty of sustaining passion and energy: 'Are you tired? Worn out? Burned out on religion? Come to me. Get away with me and you'll recover your life. I'll show you how to take a real rest. Walk with me and work with me – watch how I do it. Learn the unforced rhythms of grace. I won't lay anything heavy or ill-fitting on you. Keep company with me and you'll learn to live freely and lightly' (Matthew 11:28-30 *The Message*).

Jesus taught that our greatest priority should be to love God with all of our being and love our neighbour as ourselves (Matthew 22:36-39). Our relationship with God must be grounded in our faith in him and is strengthened by Bible reading, prayer, worship and other spiritual exercises. These practices are wellsprings that give life, direction and energy to the people, organisation and systems of The Salvation Army.

Every person linked to The Salvation Army needs to be asked where they get the energy to keep going. This is a key accountability question. Many non-Christians come with us on the journey and are attracted to our purpose. They like the way we value people. They identify with our mission and way of working. They also need energy for this journey – even if they do not recognise God as the source.

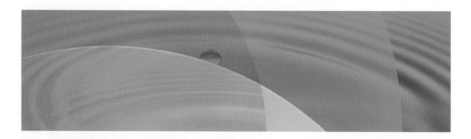

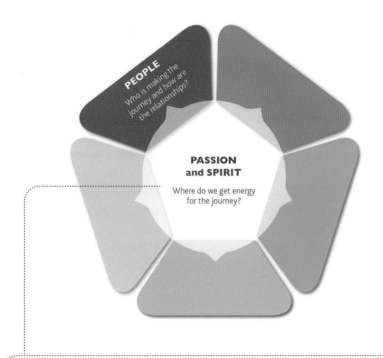

PEOPLE
Who is making the journey and how are the relationships?

PASSION
and SPIRIT

Where do we get energy
for the journey?

QUESTIONS

- Where do we get energy for the journey?
- How are our energy levels – physically, emotionally, mentally, spiritually?
- How do we sustain our passion?
- What helps us listen to the Holy Spirit?
- How do we work together? Do we use a reflective process such as FBF (see chapter 10)?

FLASHBACK: **The True Story – PASSION AND SPIRIT**

Do you remember that at a certain point in Richmond Corps' journey of renewal, Lieutenant Bram felt something was missing? The corps had moved into a new building and more people from the community were getting involved and attending Sunday meetings. However, Bram noticed that very few people were actually coming to know Jesus and experiencing real transformation in their lives. It was great to have a new and bigger building, but what would it take for that building to overflow with people being transformed by Jesus?

Bram found his answer a short time later when one night at a conference he was attending, God showed him what was missing. It was a passionate, motivating and sustaining spiritual energy that comes from only one place – prayer.

God did something special in Bram's heart that night which he said was like 'the sword of the Spirit piercing my heart and mind'. He saw that prayer was like the engine room of the Church, the place where true passion and spiritual energy for God's mission come to God's people. It is the place where God's Spirit revives, ignites, gives deeper resolve and shows us his plans.

Bram was on fire with God when he returned from the conference and over the weeks and months that followed, the whole corps caught alight. After years of inattention to the health of the corps' spiritual dynamism, something new and filled with vitality was happening.

Bible readings and songs | PASSION AND SPIRIT

Exodus 33:12-14: 'Moses said to the LORD, "You have been telling me, 'Lead these people,' but you have not let me know whom you will send with me. You have said, 'I know you by name and you have found favour with me.' If you are pleased with me, teach me your ways so I may know you and continue to find favour with you. Remember that this nation is your people." The LORD replied, "My Presence will go with you, and I will give you rest."'

Psalm 139:7-10: 'Where can I go from your Spirit? Where can I flee from your presence? If I go up to the heavens, you are there; if I make my bed in the depths, you are there. If I rise on the wings of the dawn, if I settle on the far side of the sea, even there your hand will guide me, your right hand will hold me fast.'

Luke 4:18-19: 'The Spirit of the Lord is upon me, because he has anointed me to bring good news to the poor. He has sent me to proclaim release to the captives and recovery of sight to the blind, to let the oppressed go free, to proclaim the year of the Lord's favour' (*NRSV*).

Acts 4:31: 'After they prayed, the place where they were meeting was shaken. And they were all filled with the Holy Spirit and spoke the word of God boldly.'

Romans 15:13: 'May the God of hope fill you with all joy and peace as you trust in him, so that you may overflow with hope by the power of the Holy Spirit.'

Colossians 1:28-29: 'It is he whom we proclaim, warning everyone and teaching everyone in all wisdom, so that we may present everyone mature in Christ. For this I toil and struggle with all the energy that he powerfully inspires within me' (*NRSV*).

> My Jesus, my Saviour,
> Lord, there is none like you.
> All of my days I want to praise
> The wonders of your mighty love.
> My comfort, my shelter,
> Tower of refuge and strength,
> Let every breath, all that I am,
> Never cease to worship you.
>
> *Shout to the Lord, all the earth, let us sing*
> *Power and majesty, praise to the King.*
> *Mountains bow down and the seas will roar*
> *At the sound of your name.*
> *I sing for joy at the work of your hands.*
> *Forever I'll love you, forever I'll stand.*
> *Nothing compares to the promise I have in you.*

Darlene Zschech *SASB* 264, © 1993 Wondrous Worship/MSI Music Administration

See also:
SASB 325: 'Spirit of eternal love, guide me, or I blindly rove'
SASB 430: 'Life is a journey; long is the road'
SASB 497 (v 3): 'I want, dear Lord, a soul on fire for thee'
SASB 717: 'Let the beauty of Jesus be seen in me'

 **NOTES**

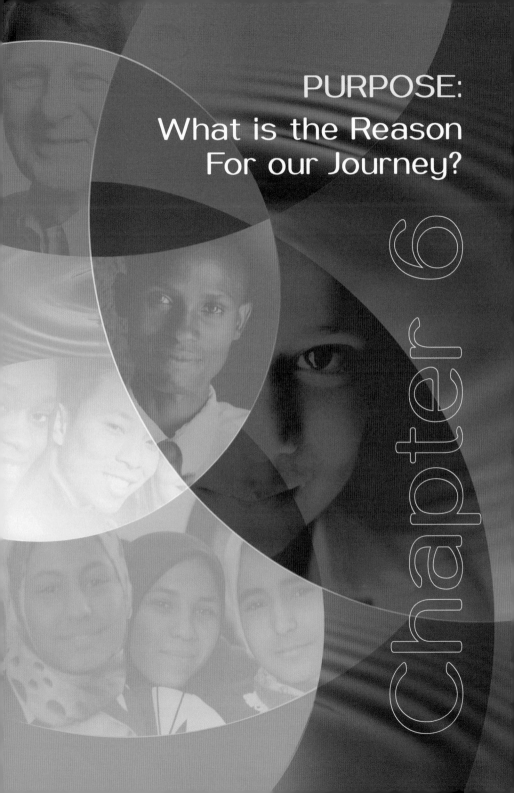

PURPOSE:
What is the Reason
For our Journey?

Chapter 6

PURPOSE:
What is the Reason
For our Journey?

People on a journey must be clear about what they intend to achieve. We need a strong and lucid purpose. It is easy to start off without being clear about the difference we want to make. Everyone serving in The Salvation Army must be able to answer the question: 'What are we trying to achieve through our work?'

This should not be a difficult question. Our purpose is not a secret – our purpose is found in our name 'The Salvation Army'. Unfortunately, not everyone appreciates the magnitude of God's salvation. Some people have a thin, narrow, incomplete understanding of salvation and focus only on 'saving souls'. Other people think The Salvation Army's purpose is only to 'help people find dignity' or 'give people their rights', but forget we are nothing without God – Father, Son and Spirit.

The Salvation Army's international mission statement describes an integrated mission: 'to preach the gospel of Jesus Christ and to meet human needs in his name without discrimination.'

The Salvation Army's *Handbook of Doctrine* (p 160) makes our purpose clear:

'All our activities, practical, social and spiritual, arise out of our basic conviction of the reality of the love of God and our desire to see all people brought into relationship with him … Our doctrine reminds us that salvation is holistic: the work of the Holy Spirit touches all areas of our life and personality, our physical, emotional and spiritual well-being, our relationships with our families and with the world around us.'

Our purpose is boundless salvation. This purpose should orientate all our plans, systems, structures, programmes and activities. The Bible emphasises the importance of having one purpose. 'Therefore, if there is any encouragement in Christ, any comfort provided by love, any fellowship in the Spirit, any affection or mercy, complete my joy and be of the same mind, by having the same love, being united in spirit, and having one purpose' (Philippians 2:1-2 *New English Translation*).

The change we seek is to achieve God's vision for his world. Song 938 in the *Song Book* describes the difference between God's vision and our purpose. Verse 1 says:

We have caught the vision splendid
Of a world which is to be,
When the pardoning love of Jesus
Freely flows from sea to sea,
When all men from strife and anger,
Greed and selfishness are free,
When the nations live together
In sweet peace and harmony.

To make this vision a reality, we need to have a clear purpose and be able to describe the desired end result. Verse 2 describes our purpose and anticipates the results:

We would help to build the city
Of our God, so wondrous fair;
Give our time, bring all our talents,
And each gift of beauty rare,
Powers of mind, and strength of purpose,
Days of labour, nights of strain,
That God's will may be accomplished,
O'er the kingdoms he shall reign.

Doris N. Rendell

All our activities should seek to bring people into relationship with God, touching all aspects of their lives, and moving them towards hope because this is God's purpose for all people, everywhere! This is boundless salvation! To be accountable, everyone must be able to explain the purpose of their work.

The MAF includes important questions that help ensure we are clear about the purpose of the journey: Why is it important to take this journey? What will change? What would happen if we did nothing?

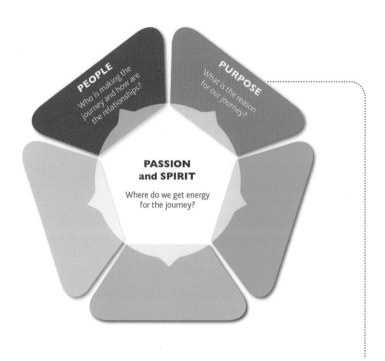

PEOPLE
Who is making the journey and how are the relationships?

PURPOSE
What is the reason for our journey?

PASSION
and SPIRIT

Where do we get energy
for the journey?

QUESTIONS

- What is the reason for our journey?
- The Salvation Army's purpose is to participate in God's mission for the world. Is there a purpose statement for this journey and does it describe what it will look like when we arrive?
- Why is it important to take this journey? What will change? What would happen if we did nothing?

FLASHBACK: **The True Story – PURPOSE**

When Lieutenants Bram and Eva arrived at Richmond Corps, there is no question that their focus was on the people – getting to know them and creating an environment where the love and healing of God could be a tangible experience. They also identified leaders and developed them.

At the same time, they started drawing attention to the corps' purpose. They knew that having a purpose was an important part of The Salvation Army's life and mission, not to mention the importance of purpose for individuals and whole groups of people. Having purpose was at the heart of also having hope and vision.

The lieutenants preached and taught on God's purpose for Richmond Corps. They had a vision for the whole Richmond community being transformed by Jesus which, of course, aligned strongly with the often stated purpose of The Salvation Army – 'The world for Christ, Christ for the world'. For the corps and its people, this purpose was about focusing on the example of Jesus who, the lieutenants would often say, helps us live, breathe and speak the values of the Kingdom of God in every part of life.

It was a refreshing message and the people of the corps began to think differently about their purpose – that God's mission was their mission, not only the officers'; that their own belief in Christ was also a call to action; that they could make a difference in the lives of others as they lived out their faith; that they needed to take responsibility for the future of the corps' mission to see Richmond transformed by Jesus.

Bible readings and songs | PURPOSE

Psalm 33:10-11: 'The LORD foils the plans of the nations; he thwarts the purposes of the peoples. But the plans of the LORD stand firm for ever, the purposes of his heart through all generations.'

John 10:9-10: 'I am the gate. Whoever enters by me will be saved, and will come in and go out and find pasture. The thief comes only to steal and kill and destroy. I came that they may have life, and have it abundantly' (*NRSV*).

1 Corinthians 3:7-9: 'So neither the one who plants nor the one who waters is anything, but only God, who makes things grow. The one who plants and the one who waters have one purpose, and they will each be rewarded according to their own labour. For we are fellow workers in God's service; you are God's field, God's building.'

2 Timothy 1:7-9: 'For the Spirit God gave us does not make us timid, but gives us power, love and self-discipline. So do not be ashamed of the testimony about our Lord or of me his prisoner. Rather, join with me in suffering for the gospel, by the power of God. He has saved us and called us to a holy life – not because of anything we have done but because of his own purpose and grace.'

O boundless salvation! deep ocean of love,
O fullness of mercy, Christ brought from above,
The whole world redeeming, so rich and so free,
Now flowing for all men, come, roll over me!

William Booth *SASB* 509 v 1

Life has no purpose unless it is yours,
Life without you has no goal;
All that fulfils me is doing your will,
Knowing that you're in control.

William Himes *SASB* 568 v 2

See also:

SASB 389: 'Rejoice! Rejoice! Christ is in you (Now is the time for us to march upon the land)'
SASB 521: 'Standing by a purpose true'
SASB 672: 'Saviour, if my feet have faltered'
SASB 858: 'I'm living my life for Jesus'
SASB 889: 'Once in misery I walked alone'

 NOTES

PLAN:
What is the Plan and How Will we Measure our Journey?

Chapter 7

PLAN:
What is the Plan and How Will we Measure our Journey?

veryone needs plans to achieve God's purpose. Moreover, we need God's plans for God's purposes. Every part of The Salvation Army needs plans that are Holy Spirit inspired, developed collaboratively, widely-owned and workable. The way we develop plans is important. Using the FBF process (see chapter 10) helps people explore the issues, participate in the planning process, reflect on the Bible and faith tradition, and seek the inspiration of the Holy Spirit. Plans will vary depending on the local context and the available resources. Tools like SMART (Specific, Measurable, Achievable, Realistic and Time-related) objectives help develop a workable, budgeted plan.

Measurable objectives are very important for accountability. We are pilgrims on a journey – we cannot wander aimlessly. We must travel with a plan and be determined to make a difference which helps achieve God's purpose. It is not adequate to plan activities and programmes without being clear about the difference that we expect. Good stewardship of mission requires us to look for and assess results.

The Salvation Army has understood the importance of measurement throughout its history. There are well-established systems to count activities (such as the number of people attending a meeting) or the output of a kitchen (such as the number of meals served).

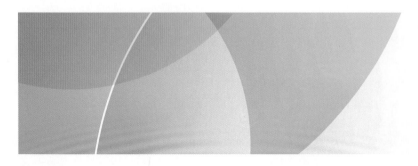

DEFINING TERMS

Activities: The actions of people linked to a Salvation Army programme that are intended to achieve the programme's purpose (e.g. the activities organised for a youth group).

Inputs: The raw materials that are used in a Salvation Army programme. These can include money, technical expertise, relationships and personnel.

Outputs: The tangible and intangible products that result from the activities of a Salvation Army programme (e.g. the number of meals served at a disaster site).

Outcomes: The benefits that a Salvation Army programme is designed to deliver (e.g. the number of young people who become junior soldiers as a result of the Sunday school programme).

Impact measurement: A process involving tools used to measure the difference a programme makes on a specific person, group of people or specific location. The definition of impact depends specifically on the goals and the issues being addressed.

It is complex to measure an outcome or the impact of a Salvation Army programme. How do we measure the outcome of a sermon on a congregation or the impact over three years of a corps officer's ministry? Although these are difficult concepts to measure, when we understand outcomes and impact we are equipped to exercise good judgement in assessing progress on our journey and making decisions about modifying programmes to ensure greater effectiveness.

It is critical to the ongoing success of a plan that we are committed to measuring the difference being made in the lives of people. Not every Salvation Army corps/centre/headquarters will be ready to measure the 'impact' of its mission and associated programmes. Some may be making progress if they start accurately measuring 'inputs' and 'outputs'. Others may already be competent in measurement and therefore ready to try to measure more complex factors such as outcomes and, perhaps, even impact. What is important is ensuring there is a credible plan to collect and use reliable measurement information.

The Salvation Army Measurement Framework

The Salvation Army Measurement Framework is a people-focused framework. It assesses two aspects of people's lives – contextual factors and relational factors.

FOUR CONTEXTUAL FACTORS

There are four contextual factors which affect the quality of life of every person. These are:

- Protection/Safety

- Well-being/Health

- Formation/Education

- Service/Work

Every expression of Salvation Army ministry can use one or more of these four contextual factors to develop its plan by asking: What aspects of a person's life will this programme improve? What measurement tools can we use?

The One Army Impact Initiative developed examples of outcomes that can be sought in people's lives in their context:

PROTECTION/SAFETY

This outcome will be achieved when: Children and adults are free from abuse, discrimination, hunger, homelessness and fear, and find sanctuary and security in their lives.

Reflection: Isaiah 40:31

'Those who hope in the LORD will renew their strength. They will soar on wings like eagles; they will run and not grow weary, they will walk and not be faint.'

WELL-BEING/HEALTH

This outcome will be achieved when: Children and adults live well. This includes people's physical, mental, social and spiritual well-being as they seek a life that is in harmony with God, with each other and all creation.

Reflection: John 10:10

'I have come that they may have life, and have it to the full.'

FORMATION/EDUCATION

This outcome will be achieved when: Children and adults develop into compassionate people of integrity and character with relevant skills, knowledge and understanding to achieve their full God-given potential.

Reflection: Mark 8:34

'Whoever wants to be my disciple must deny themselves and take up their cross and follow me.'

SERVICE/WORK

This outcome will be achieved when: Wherever children and adults are – at home, school, field, factory, office, church or community – their time, talents and abilities are able to be used in work and service.

Reflection: John 9:4

'As long as it is day, we must do the work of him who sent me.'

The local context is very important when measuring progress. For example, teachers working in Salvation Army schools in India and Kenya are educating children in very different contexts. They should not have standardised measurement indicators imposed on them – the measurement tools need to be relevant to the context.

THREE RELATIONAL FACTORS

It is also important for every Salvation Army programme to plan to strengthen relationships. The Bible is full of teaching about the importance of relational characteristics. Paul, writing to the church at Galatia, listed some of them: 'The fruit of the spirit is love, joy, peace, patience, kindness, generosity, faithfulness, gentleness, and self-control' (Galatians 5:22-23 *NRSV*). The life of Jesus exemplified other characteristics we should seek in our relationships – hope, trust, justice, hospitality, truthfulness, resilience and courage.

Measuring relationships is not easy. We know from our personal experience that while we instinctively know if we have more hope or trust in a relationship, it is not easy to give it a reliable grade. However, measuring relationships is not the main aim

– the priority is to ensure our plans include activities which prioritise, develop and sustain good relationships. Wherever possible, progress should be measurable.

Stories and testimonies are a proven Salvation Army way to assess how our relationships with God, each other and the world around us are progressing. Building time and space into the plan for sharing stories and reflecting on progress is important.

It is not easy to scientifically prove relational outcomes, but we all know them when we see them. As noted earlier, the priority is to seek for more hope, love and trust in all relationships in all Salvation Army programmes.

'We remember before our God and Father your work produced by faith, your labour prompted by love, and your endurance inspired by hope in our Lord Jesus Christ' (1 Thessalonians 1:3).

HOPE

This outcome will be achieved when: God is our source of hope for the future. This hope gives us strength, energy, inspiration and joy for the journey.
Reflection: Romans 8:24; Romans 5:5; Acts 26:6.

LOVE

This outcome will be achieved when: Love is experienced as a gift from God. This love can be the foundation of all relationships, restoration, reconciliation and redemption.
Reflection: Proverbs 3:5; 1 Corinthians chapter 13.

TRUST

This outcome will be achieved when: Faith in God is the foundation of trust. Trust binds us in relationship with God and others as we seek transformation in our lives and communities.
Reflection: John 15:9.

The Accountability Movement encourages each part of The Salvation Army to use a plan that is effective, efficient and faithful. The MAF includes the important question: 'Is the plan communicated effectively and owned by all those involved?'

As 'One Army' we can learn much from each other. International and territorial policies, strategies and positional statements give important direction. Beyond the Army, we can gain insights from considering international and national strategies such as the Sustainable Development Goals (2016 to 2030) agreed by all 193 countries who comprise the United Nations. Therefore the MAF asks: 'Is the plan in line with any relevant international or territorial policies, strategies and positional statements?'

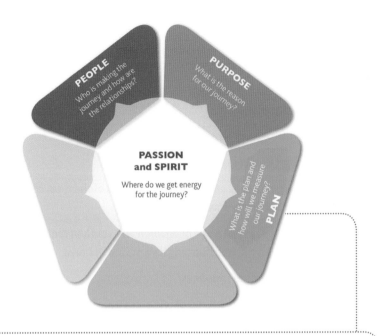

QUESTIONS

- What is the plan and how will we measure our journey?
- Is the plan communicated effectively and owned by all those involved?
- Is the plan in line with any relevant international or territorial strategies?
- What outcomes are expected on the journey? (A list of activities and programmes is not enough.)

FLASHBACK: The True Story – PLAN

How crucial it is to have a plan. Most people would be aware of the saying based on Proverbs 29:18, 'Where there is no vision, the people perish' (*King James Version*). Well, we can justifiably add to that, 'Without a plan, people drift!'

The whole story of Richmond Corps, as shared in chapter 1, is a journey of renewal that involved a plan and course of action right from the start. Lieutenants Bram and Eva arrived fresh out of the officer training college and within a month had identified issues that needed to be addressed if the corps was to flourish and grow. These issues all revolved around poor stewardship and a lacklustre accountability.

A plan of action focusing on greater accountability evolved, with a number of main points:

- Building healthy relationships
- Developing healthy and passionate spirituality
- Identifying and developing leaders
- Understanding the needs and specific personality of the local community and therefore the context for mission
- Understanding the special place of children and youth in the heart of God, and reaching them with the transforming love of God in Christ
- Being better stewards of resources
- Being creative in the stewardship of resources by taking better care of Army property, paying tithes and improving corps income-generating activities
- Inspiring a new sense of purpose and ownership in mission
- Seeking and following God's plan always, being flexible, ready for surprises and ready to adjust.

The lieutenants and the people of Richmond Corps were faithful and passionate in following this emerging plan and the results spoke for themselves.

Bible readings and songs | PLAN

Proverbs 19:21: 'The human mind may devise many plans, but it is the purpose of the Lord that will be established' (*NRSV*).

Jeremiah 29:4-7, 10-11: 'Thus says the Lord of hosts, the God of Israel, to all the exiles whom I have sent into exile from Jerusalem to Babylon: Build houses and live in them; plant gardens and eat what they produce. Take wives and have sons and daughters; take wives for your sons, and give your daughters in marriage, that they may bear sons and daughters; multiply there, and do not decrease. But seek the welfare of the city where I have sent you into exile, and pray to the Lord on its behalf, for in its welfare you will find your welfare ... For thus says the Lord: Only when Babylon's seventy years are completed will I visit you, and I will fulfil to you my promise and bring you back to this place. For surely I know the plans I have for you, says the Lord, plans for your welfare and not for harm, to give you a future with hope' (*NRSV*).

Luke 14:27-30: 'Whoever does not carry the cross and follow me cannot be my disciple. For which of you, intending to build a tower, does not first sit down and estimate the cost, to see whether he has enough to complete it? Otherwise, when he has laid a foundation and is not able to finish, all who see it will begin to ridicule him, saying, "This fellow began to build and was not able to finish"' (*NRSV*).

Philippians 3:13-14: 'Brothers and sisters, I do not consider myself yet to have taken hold of it. But one thing I do: forgetting what is behind and straining towards what is ahead, I press on towards the goal to win the prize for which God has called me heavenwards in Christ Jesus.'

Teach me to dance to the beat of your heart,
Teach me to move in the power of your Spirit,
Teach me to walk in the light of your presence,
Teach me to dance to the beat of your heart.
Teach me to love with your heart of compassion,
Teach me to trust in the word of your promise,
Teach me to hope in the day of your coming,
Teach me to dance to the beat of your heart.

Graham Kendrick and Steve Thompson *SASB* 392 © 1993 Gateway Music

See also:
SASB 321: 'I dare to live the life of faith'
SASB 342 (v 2): 'Except you build the house, Lord'
SASB 355: 'Beautiful Lord, wonderful Saviour (The Potter's Hand)'
SASB 857 (v 3): 'I'm going to turn my life into an active quest'
SASB 926 (v 2): 'Fill us with thy Holy Spirit'

NOTES

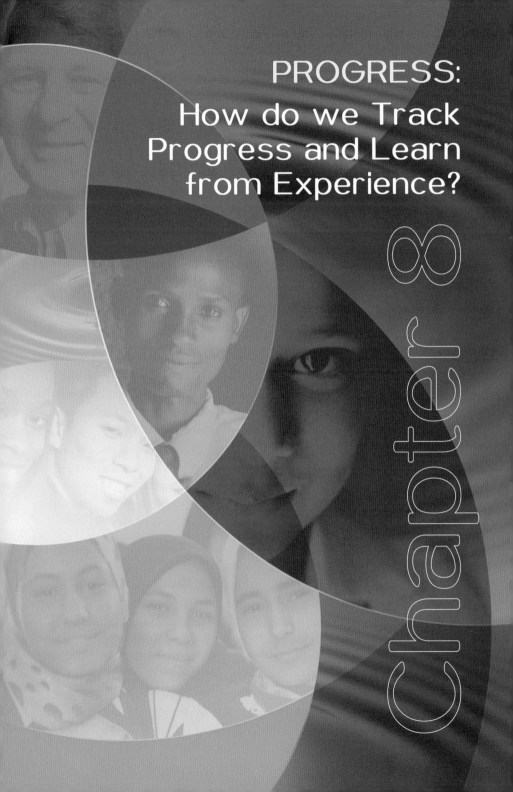

PROGRESS:
How do we Track Progress and Learn from Experience?

Chapter 8

8

PROGRESS:
How do we Track Progress and Learn from Experience?

As we journey towards the purpose we need to track progress and learn from experience. There is no point in doing the same thing year after year and not making any progress towards the purpose. Neither is there any point in assessing the effectiveness of our plan if we don't implement changes to the plan when it is failing to make the difference in people's lives we had originally envisaged. That is demoralising and frustrating for everyone. Using the MAF gives opportunities to track the difference we are making and make changes when required. Everything we do should help achieve our purpose.

The Salvation Army has always measured activities and programmes using statistics. It is important to continue collecting statistics on activities and programmes. We need to know what resources are being used (inputs). It is important to know what outputs are being produced by our work (for example the number of people served a meal or the number of people attending a Sunday morning meeting).

It is also important to understand the long-term difference being made in people's lives – the social, spiritual, physical, economic and environmental outcomes and

CASE STUDY

A report sent to IHQ from a territory in India stated that young people were organised by a corps to participate in a blood donor programme. The report included a picture showing many young people taking part – but no specific number was reported. The number of pints of blood was not measured (the output); and there was no attempt to measure the number of lives saved (outcome). Neither was there any data collected on the impact of the blood donor programme on the donors. Improved measurement tools will help the young people understand the difference they are making and may encourage other people to donate blood.

impact. The Salvation Army will be more faithful and dynamic in mission when we understand the difference we are making and, with that information, learn, adapt and improve.

A key aspect of the Accountability Movement is encouraging each part of The Salvation Army to have regular accountability discussions to review progress. The MAF is designed as a self-assessment tool. While it is expected that our leaders will use the MAF during reviews and audits, it can be used by individuals and local teams to track progress, monitor the implementation of the plan, review the statistics to ensure they are outcome measures, and then to see if the outcomes are being achieved, learn from experience and change plans where necessary.

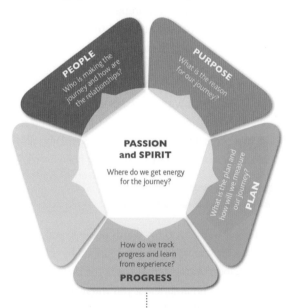

QUESTIONS

- How do we track progress and learn from experience?
- What measurement tools are used to track progress?
- How do we use the measurement information to adapt and learn from experience?
- Is the progress in line with the purpose, plan and budget?

FLASHBACK: The True Story – PROGRESS

Did you notice in chapter 1 that monitoring progress and adjusting their approach towards God's purpose was key to Richmond Corps flourishing on their journey of renewal? The corps officers, new leadership team and corps itself became accountable for progress. When things weren't going the way they felt they should be, the corps officers and leadership team particularly would ask themselves why, actively seek answers, and then implement those answers as they came to light.

A big change happened when they realised, starting with Lieutenant Bram, that the corps did not have enough love for God and that true Godly passion and energy was missing among them. Such a lack was impeding their journey of renewal. As we have noted already, it was then that they realised the mission of God was a spiritual mission requiring spiritual energy and dynamism.

They discovered that such energy came from only one place – prayer. Prayer became a 24/7 reality among them and suddenly things took off, including the passion of corps members for sharing Jesus with others, the number of people finding new life and hope in Jesus, worship meetings being filled with a new and refreshing sense of the presence of God, and corps finances growing exponentially, allowing the corps to venture out with new mission initiatives that had long been overdue.

Bible readings and songs | PROGRESS

John 15:7-12: 'If you abide in me, and my words abide in you, ask for whatever you wish, and it will be done for you. My Father is glorified by this, that you bear much fruit and become my disciples. As the Father has loved me, so I have loved you; abide in my love. If you keep my commandments, you will abide in my love, just as I have kept my Father's commandments and abide in his love. I have said these things to you so that my joy may be in you, and that your joy may be complete. This is my commandment, that you love one another as I have loved you' (*NRSV*).

Galatians 5:22-26: 'The fruit of the Spirit is love, joy, peace, patience, kindness, generosity, faithfulness, gentleness, and self-control. There is no law against such things. And those who belong to Christ Jesus have crucified the flesh with its passions and desires. If we live by the Spirit, let us also be guided by the Spirit. Let us not become conceited, competing against one another, envying one another' (*NRSV*).

Philippians 1:9-11: 'And this is my prayer, that your love may overflow more and more with knowledge and full insight to help you to determine what is best, so that on the day of Christ you may be pure and blameless, having produced the harvest of righteousness that comes through Jesus Christ for the glory and praise of God' (*NRSV*).

Colossians 1:3-6, 9-10: 'In our prayers for you we always thank God, the Father of our Lord Jesus Christ, for we have heard of your faith in Christ Jesus and of the love that you have for all the saints, because of the hope laid up for you in heaven. You have heard of this hope before in the word of the truth, the gospel that has come to you. Just as it is bearing fruit and growing in the whole world, so it has been bearing fruit among yourselves from the day you heard it and truly comprehended the grace of God ... For this reason, since the day we heard it, we have not ceased praying for you and asking that you may be filled with the knowledge of God's will in all spiritual wisdom and understanding, so that you may lead lives worthy of the Lord, fully pleasing to him, as you bear fruit in every good work and as you grow in the knowledge of God' (*NRSV*).

Lord, I come to you,
Let my heart be changed, renewed,
Flowing from the grace that I found in you.
And Lord, I've come to know
The weaknesses I see in me
Will be stripped away by the power of your love.

Hold me close,
Let your love surround me.
Bring me near, draw me to your side.
And as I wait, I'll rise up like the eagle,
And I will soar with you,
Your Spirit leads me on in the power of your love.

Geoff Bullock *SASB* 601 © 1992 Word Music

See also:

SASB 278 (v 2): 'Happy, still in God confiding'
SASB 305: 'Now the fruit of the Spirit is patience'
SASB 926 (v 3): 'Give us all more holy living'
SASB 971: 'Onward, Christian soldiers'
SASB 991 (v 3): 'His Kingdom cometh not by force'

 NOTES

PROCEDURES AND SYSTEMS:
Are They Fit For Purpose?

Chapter 9

PROCEDURES AND SYSTEMS:
Are They Fit For Purpose?

The sixth dimension in the MAF checks that every procedure and system is fit for purpose. During the One Army Accountability Review many territories reported concerns about the effectiveness and efficiency of Salvation Army procedures and systems. They are not always serving the mission; some are seen to be holding people back on the journey.

The Salvation Army must have systems for the 21st-century journey that are fit for our God-given purpose. This includes systems such as governance, management, personnel, safeguarding, measurement, finance and property. If our systems compromise God's purposes, we are failing people and we are failing God.

The Salvation Army has many existing systems. They must be regularly reviewed to ensure they are fit for God's purpose and truly support us on the journey. Procedures and systems are important in ensuring we are faithful, accountable and achieve quality. One expected outcome of the Accountability Movement is a reduction in bureaucracy across The Salvation Army. Cutting bureaucracy will be possible if systems serve our God-given purpose.

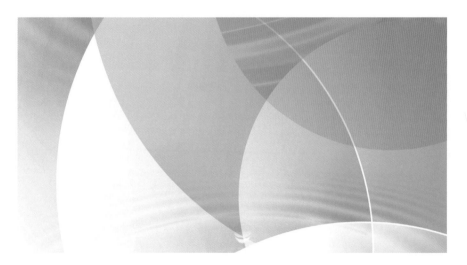

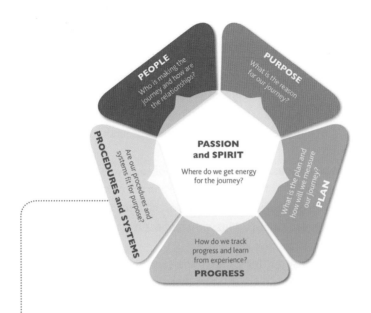

The diagram shows five segments around a central hub:

PEOPLE — Who is making the journey and how are the relationships?

PURPOSE — What is the reason for our journey?

PLAN — What is the plan and how will we measure our journey?

PROGRESS — How do we track progress and learn from experience?

PROCEDURES and SYSTEMS — Are our procedures and systems fit for purpose?

PASSION and SPIRIT — Where do we get energy for the journey?

QUESTIONS

- Are our procedures and systems fit for purpose?

- Are all our dealings (purchasing, finance, property, personnel, client services, decision-making) conducted in line with Kingdom values?

- Is the work being done in accordance with national and local laws? Are all relevant professional standards being implemented?

- Are Salvation Army policies (orders and regulations, memorandums of appointment, briefs of appointment and job descriptions) accessible, implemented and reviewed appropriately?

- Is an appropriate risk management system in place?

FLASHBACK: The True Story – PROCEDURES AND SYSTEMS

Lieutenants Bram and Eva, from our story in chapter 1, were not the kind of officers who ignore Salvation Army procedures and systems. For example, they followed procedure when, after talking with the corps people, they told THQ it was time to spend money on a new corps building, and it was urgent.

The divisional leaders were keen to help. They sent a team from divisional headquarters (DHQ) to conduct an audit of the current building and survey the town for any appropriate land that might be available. The DHQ team also looked at the corps' finances and devised a scheme based on what might be affordable, using proceeds from the sale of the existing property, local corps fundraising efforts and a grant and loan from THQ.

A new property was purchased on the other side of town where there was much housing development. The corps followed procedure and there was a good result. But for the lieutenants, other procedures and methods of the Army seemed cumbersome and overbearing. They had to come to grips with this because it became clear that the Army was not going to change overnight.

With the increase in finances that came to the corps through people's increased giving and a revamped Red Shield Family Store that saw profits more than double in the space of a few months, the corps hired a secretary to handle all the paperwork.

This resulted in freeing up the lieutenants to attend to the increasing complexity of corps life when there are many more people in your 'flock'. They devised their own procedures and a system that worked well within the greater Salvation Army system. It also gave them a little more space for themselves and their family, and enabled them to work on themselves and their own development as leaders. By working with a supportive DHQ, the lieutenants ensured that Richmond Corps' procedures and systems were fit for purpose and helped enhance mission effectiveness.

Bible readings and songs | PROCEDURES AND SYSTEMS

Ecclesiastes 8:5-6: 'Whoever obeys his command will come to no harm, and the wise heart will know the proper time and procedure. For there is a proper time and procedure for every matter.'

Luke 16:10-13: 'Whoever is faithful in a very little is faithful also in much; and whoever is dishonest in a very little is dishonest also in much. If then you have not been faithful with the dishonest wealth, who will entrust to you the true riches? And if you have not been faithful with what belongs to another, who will give you what is your own? No slave can serve two masters; for a slave will either hate the one and love the other, or be devoted to the one and despise the other. You cannot serve God and wealth' (*NRSV*).

1 Corinthians 4:1-2: 'Think of us in this way, as servants of Christ and stewards of God's mysteries. Moreover, it is required of stewards that they should be found trustworthy' (*NRSV*).

Titus 1:7-9: 'For a bishop, as God's steward, must be blameless; he must not be arrogant or quick-tempered or addicted to wine or violent or greedy for gain; but he must be hospitable, a lover of goodness, prudent, upright, devout, and self-controlled. He must have a firm grasp of the word that is trustworthy in accordance with the teaching, so that he may be able both to preach with sound doctrine and to refute those who contradict it' (*NRSV*).

> Leave no unguarded place,
> No weakness of the soul;
> Take every virtue, every grace,
> And fortify the whole.

Charles Wesley *SASB* 979 v 3

> Arm me with jealous care,
> As in thy sight to live;
> And O thy servant, Lord, prepare
> A strict account to give!

Charles Wesley *SASB* 946 v 3

See also:

SASB 940 (v 2): 'We're an Army brave, arrayed in armour bright'
SASB 959 (v 2): 'I'll go in the strength of the Lord to work he appoints me to do'

 NOTES

Answering Questions Together –
Using Faith-Based Facilitation

Chapter 10

Answering Questions Together – Using Faith-Based Facilitation

A
S we have seen in the previous chapters, the MAF uses a process to explore important questions in six key areas. It can be used in all parts of The Salvation Army – in rural areas and cities, in corps and social centres, from health services in remote villages in Kenya or Bangladesh to employment services in some of the world's largest metropolises. The questions can be addressed by individuals and teams, or whole territories and divisions.

Many of the questions cannot be answered easily or quickly, so this chapter on Faith-Based Facilitation (FBF) is provided to help us explore the questions in a meaningful way that will hopefully produce significant Kingdom outcomes right where you are.

FBF is a process that many Salvationists are already using. For example, the United Kingdom Territory with the Republic of Ireland encourages the use of FBF in corps and centres as well as in communities to analyse what is happening, to reflect on this in the light of faith and work out an action plan. FBF is also used by many Salvationists in Africa, the Caribbean, South America and Asia to think through issues in their context. Obviously, the outcomes of the process are different in different parts of the world.

Everyone can use the FBF process to structure conversations and help people think, talk, explore and respond to their issues in the light of faith. Using the process results in the development of healthier people and communities who enjoy deeper relationships. It is not a tool, theory or a project in itself – it is a way of working, a way of thinking, a way of living, a way of being.

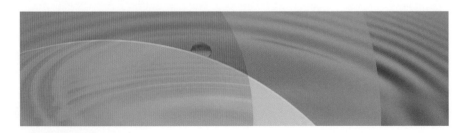

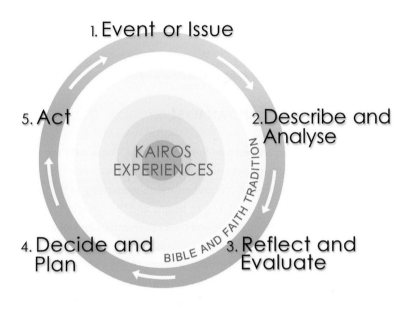

1. **Event or Issue**

5. **Act**

2. **Describe and Analyse**

KAIROS
EXPERIENCES

FAITH TRADITION

4. **Decide and Plan**

BIBLE AND

3. **Reflect and Evaluate**

This diagram shows the different elements of the FBF process. Let's see how it works and how we can apply it to the questions asked in the MAF.

EVENT OR ISSUE

The process starts when people identify an issue that needs to be reviewed to see what we are doing, why we are doing it, and how we could do it much better. In terms of the MAF, this step is easy for us in one sense, because the issue to be reviewed is the question the MAF puts to us. For example, the first question asked in the MAF is: Who is making the journey and how are the relationships? This question, and the subset of questions that follows, is about the health of people and their relationships. This is the issue to be explored and you can use FBF to help answer the questions.

Have a general discussion about the question(s) before going deeper in Steps 2 and 3. Should you take the questions through the FBF process as a block or one by one?

Remember, throughout the FBF process it is important that people participate in an environment in which:

- They feel safe and encouraged to share,
- There is mutual respect for each other's perspectives, insights, experience and gifts,
- Learning from each other and from God is a core value.

FBF | STEP 2   DESCRIBE AND ANALYSE

The MAF questions are then analysed as fully as possible. Those who are reflecting (together or individually) try to think of every factor that has influenced the subject of the questions. This builds a deep and comprehensive understanding of the experience so far. So in terms of the questions relating to people and their relationships, you try and pinpoint the level of health in people and their relationships and what has and is impacting their health.

It is important not to arrive at superficial answers to the MAF questions. Be as objective as possible. Keep carefully to description and analysis and avoid judgements and opinion. Brainstorming would be helpful here, where everyone's ideas are recorded on a blackboard, whiteboard or flipchart, or a large piece of paper. Some prioritising might need to follow.

FBF | STEP 3   REFLECT AND EVALUATE

This step of the process involves thinking through the factors that have emerged, and sharing ideas and responses. Continuing the example from Steps 1 and 2, if the subject and the questions being addressed are about the health of the person/corps/centre/team and the people's relationships, it will be vital to talk through the reasons for what came up in Step 2 and how those involved can grow in the quality of their relationships and in the experience of all people sharing the vision and feeling accepted.

People of faith will find reading Scripture, prayer and quiet reflection to be helpful activities between Steps 2 and 3. It is at this step that careful evaluation is made, and tough questions need to be asked and answered. For example: How far does this person/corps/centre/team remain true to its original aims and values? What insights or events or teaching from the Bible connect with this situation? What needs to be changed to make this situation better and of greater value for all concerned?

During this time of reflection and evaluation, it may be that a Kairos experience (see 'Kairos Experiences' below) emerges. Such experiences cannot be predicted or ordered, but are unlikely to happen unless the participants are in an open and receptive frame of mind. As well as time for prayer and reflection, taking time out, or engaging in a 'creative thinking' activity, may result in greater receptivity.

Evaluation and reflection should never be rushed, and certainly never missed out! The major part of the time spent working through the FBF process needs to be spent on this step.

FBF | STEP 4   DECIDE AND PLAN

A well-facilitated time of reflection using the FBF process will usually lead to decisions the participants can own and put into practice; for example, a plan for increasing the health of the person/corps/centre/team and their relationships.

If it proves difficult to reach agreement it can be helpful to make a list of all possible options for action. Groups or individuals can then list the positives and negatives of each option. As these are shared in the larger group it may be that agreement will begin to emerge. Sometimes it may be difficult to reach complete agreement in a group for a particular course of action. If this happens it will be necessary for the facilitator to bring the group to a majority decision, seeking as much consensus as possible.

Identifying strengths and resources is important at this step to ensure that it will be possible to carry out the decisions made. Prioritising will be helpful in deciding between a number of possible options. To make sure that the agreed decision is acted upon, it is helpful to ask:

- What resources are available to implement the plan? How will the gaps be filled?
- Who will be responsible for each of the agreed plans and when will they be carried out?
- What training and/or support may be needed?

- What safeguards need to be included?
- How should problems be approached?
- Who needs to be told about the plans and who will let them know?
- When will progress be reviewed?

FBF | STEP 5   TAKE ACTION

Translating decisions into action is vital. Remember to list the action points, assess the impact of the action and collect appropriate information.

This will be needed during the next cycle steps 2 and 3. And then it continues: the FBF process does not stop at the last step, but continues on and on. After Step 5 Action, the changes made will lead to a new FBF cycle:

A NEW STEP 1   EVENT OR ISSUE

The action taken resulting from this process will lead to transformation and so there will be a 'new experience' at Step 1.

A NEW STEP 2   DESCRIBE AND ANALYSE

A new description and analysis of the changed situation will be needed. (It is important to do this carefully. You may be surprised to discover how many changes the action has brought about.)

A NEW STEP 3   REFLECT AND EVALUATE

This is the vital point where the changes brought about by the action can be reflected on and evaluated. It is essential to do this before continuing with any further action. It may be helpful to take a break at this step, to see what impact the action already taken may have in the longer term.

KEEPING THE FAITH

In addition to contemporary contextual evidence, FBF identifies three important influences that The Salvation Army uses in shaping policy:

1. The Bible,

2. The tradition of the Church,

3. The inspiration of God in the 'Kairos experience'.

People of faith are influenced by the teachings handed down through the generations. The Salvation Army, as a Christian church, believes that the Scriptures of the Old and New Testament were given by inspiration of God and that they offer essential, divine guidance that helps people live life to the full.

The Salvation Army does not give the same authority to the tradition of the Church as it gives to the Bible. However, we recognise that there is much to learn from the experience and teachings of Christians who have gone before, and therefore the lessons learnt and patterns established by faith tradition should be analysed and reflected upon as they will often provide valuable insight.

KAIROS EXPERIENCES

Unexpected ideas can occur at any step of the FBF process but especially during the times of reflection, evaluation and decision. People of faith can often sense God at work in these moments. A 'Kairos experience' is the term used to describe these occasions.

There is a well-known example of a Kairos experience in Salvation Army history when William Booth said to his wife, Catherine, when returning home after a meeting in the East End of London: 'Darling, I have found my destiny.' He felt God leading him in a particular way. William Booth had a Kairos experience.

The Gospel of Matthew records that Peter, one of the disciples who had been with Jesus for a couple of years, eventually recognised who Jesus was and said: 'You are the Christ, the Son of the living God' (Matthew 16:16 *English Standard Version*). Jesus told many stories about people having unexpected ideas, such as the prodigal son (Luke 15:11-32) when the young man 'came to his senses' (v 17) after a number of bad experiences and a long time of reflection. It was a Kairos experience that led to a wonderful reunion with his father.

Kairos is a Greek word (καιρος) that isn't easy to translate into other languages – it means something like 'God's moment' or 'the right time'. Such flashes of inspiration may come when we are not actively seeking them. New insight may also happen gradually and not necessarily at a specifically defined 'moment'. FBF understands these experiences to be the work of God. Christians find the Bible, prayer and times of reflection can stimulate and lead to a Kairos experience.

'Kairos experiences' has been placed at the centre of the FBF diagram to indicate the presence and influence of God in all aspects of life. It reminds people of faith of the importance of always integrating beliefs with actions and the promise that God is always present.

 NOTES

Shifting Culture

Chapter 11

Shifting Culture

Seeing the Accountability Movement flourish across 127 countries requires renewed vision and momentum in every place. It will not happen just because the General wants it to happen. It needs everyone to get involved in every part of The Salvation Army. You do not need to wait for anyone to give you permission to be accountable. You can start to use the MAF immediately to help you enter into the journey of renewal. Look at the questions – what is God challenging you about?

When the review of accountability in The Salvation Army commenced in 2013, the leaders in all territories and commands were asked for their views. As noted on page 25, 93 per cent responded and the main concerns surrounded ineffective systems and poor relationships between people. Therefore, the focus is on strengthening the systems and improving our relationships.

Strengthening Army systems

In January 2015, the General's Consultative Council considered all the work done by the One Army Impact Initiative and the One Army Accountability Review. It was decided The Salvation Army needs an integrated Accountability Movement with four main pillars: governance, impact measurement, finance and child protection, supported by leadership development, capacity building and communication.

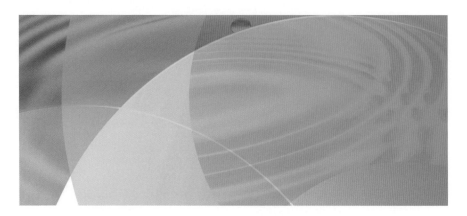

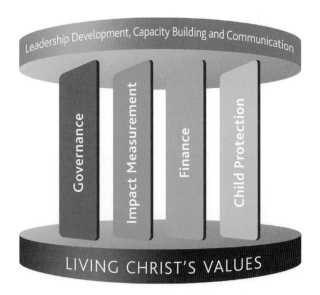

Each pillar has a purpose statement:

- **Governance:** To ensure, at all levels, The Salvation Army has a governance structure fit for its God-given purpose in the 21st century.

- **Impact Measurement:** To increase the transformative change The Salvation Army works towards with people and communities through measurement and learning.

- **Finance:** To monitor, review, upgrade and enhance worldwide Salvation Army financial systems to develop sector-leading practice, ensure wide-ranging stakeholder accountability, facilitate capacity building of finance personnel and enable funding for purpose.

- **Child Protection:** To ensure The Salvation Army's commitment to the well-being and protection of children by implementing best practice in every expression of Salvation Army contact and influence with children. (While The Salvation Army recognises its duty to safeguard every person under its influence, the Accountability Movement is initially prioritising the protection of children.)

The four pillars – plus leadership development, capacity building and communication – are key elements of the Accountability Movement. All are built on the platform of living Christ's values. This ambitious change programme will be overseen by the Chief of the Staff.

Changing the culture

This is the biggest challenge! There is no doubt that there are many differences in our 'One Army'. At times, even talking about 'One Army' seems unrealistic. How can we compare ministry in New York City, USA, with Army work on a remote Indonesian island? However, we have much more in common than we often appreciate. In every country, The Salvation Army works with people who – like ourselves – live in an imperfect, fallen world. Most importantly, we all depend on the same Saviour and Holy Spirit who give us grace, wisdom and energy to serve.

A review of accountability concerns across the Army resulted in the same issues being repeatedly raised:

- Poor relationships between fellow officers,

- A lack of financial integrity,

- Poor stewardship of resources,

- A lack of trust between officers and soldiers,

- Distrust between corps, centres and headquarters,

- Sexual failings,

- People seeking personal power for personal benefit,

- A lack of love for people who are different to us,

- Out-of-date procedures and systems which are not fit for the Army's 21st-century mission.

General André Cox is driving the process forward at IHQ, but he has admitted he cannot do that for every territory or command. Territory and command leaders need to lead the change process in their areas of responsibility. Division, centre and corps leaders need to support the change process where they are.

However, we will not achieve the change God wants in The Salvation Army if we only focus on fixing systems. We also need to be brave and address relational problems. Why do we allow poor relationships or the abuse of power by some leaders in our corps, centres and headquarters to go unchallenged? Yes, we are a hierarchical organisation. Yes, we do need to accept authority, but as the General has said: 'Authority is entrusted to an individual for the purpose of the common good within the community' (see 1 Kings 3:9; 1 Corinthians 12:7).

Power can be used in many ways. It is not just hierarchical power and authority that can be used for the common good. There are many opportunities for people to use personal influence for the Kingdom. Influence does not depend on a person's position in life, or on rank if you are a Salvation Army officer. Can you think of a person who has influence that far exceeds their position or rank? Of course, influence can be used negatively and frustrate God's purposes. Any authority, power or influence we have in The Salvation Army is not for our personal benefit. If we use our position for selfish ends, we need to be held to account for our unfaithfulness.

For the Accountability Movement to gain momentum, every one linked to The Salvation Army – employees, junior and senior soldiers, active and retired officers, adherents, volunteers, friends – needs to catch the vision and get involved. This is a huge communications challenge. People don't get excited by accountability! As we have already noted, it can make people defensive or nervous.

However, the vast majority of our Army family will be inspired and convinced if they see that leaders – both officers and non-officers – are personally committed to greater accountability. Our people long to see the Army being more effective in God's mission. We will quickly become cynical and demotivated if we sense that this is just a pretence to keep the General happy. This is not his idea!

At the Last Supper, Jesus encouraged his disciples: 'A new command I give you: love one another. As I have loved you, so you must love one another. By this everyone will know that you are my disciples, if you love one another' (John 13:34-35). So what does 'love one another' look like in practice for a 21st-century Salvation Army? This may well be different from some of the attitudes and culture we have accepted in the past.

For example:
● **Let us move away from a culture of 'why do they need to know?' towards an open, transparent culture of 'why shouldn't people be told?'** People can be trusted

with more information – especially about finances and stewardship of resources. Obviously there is often a need for pastoral confidentiality, but this should not be an excuse to sweep sin or mediocrity under the carpet.

● **Let us move away from a culture of 'don't ask difficult questions' to encouraging people to think, discuss and debate how the Army can be more effective, efficient and faithful in doing God's will in our communities.** We are not being loyal to God or the Army when we look the other way and 'suffer in silence', as one African officer described this problem recently. A strong leader allows people to disagree but is able to explain the reasons for a decision. A weak leader silences all disagreement often by abusing power.

● **Let us reject a culture of 'we must protect the reputation of the Army at all costs' – even if that means hiding the truth.** At times we need to confront sin or unacceptable situations, even if people misunderstand our actions. These situations are often personally very costly. The Salvation Army is a highly trusted organisation, but we cannot take that trust for granted. We need to continually build trust in our communities by being people of integrity – despite the cost.

● **Let us reject a culture of distrust and encourage an attitude of mutual respect and truth-telling between Army leaders and those under their command.** Too many officers and soldiers presume senior leaders are incompetent or corrupt, or both. Are we taking on the attitudes of the world where all leaders are distrusted – in government, business, the law, medicine and the Church? Is this culture of distrust infecting relationships in the Army?

We do not have to be close friends with everyone, but we need to work together for God's mission. The players from winning sports teams often refer to the importance of their team values. Players who do not buy into the team culture are dropped. If athletes recognise the importance of this to becoming a sports champion, how much more should we be willing to live out Christ's values in 'Team' Salvation Army?

Developing a culture of trust and mutual respect means that if leaders or followers behave badly there must be consequences. The General has made it clear that everyone needs to be held to account – failings need to be addressed and robust reporting systems are required.

However, we need to trust our leaders unless there is evidence to the contrary. We should give them the benefit of our doubts and at the same time be brave enough to tell them what we are thinking. Our leaders should respond to our opinions with grace and honesty. Where there is evidence of failure, we must find ways to address the problem inside the Army. We can remind ourselves of Paul's strong words to the church at Corinth (1 Corinthians 6:1-11) before considering other courses of action. Let us reject the practice of complaining secretly or writing anonymous letters.

We need to learn how to 'speak the truth in love' (Ephesians 4:15) to each other. A new accountability culture will require effective processes to address the concerns of whistle-blowers – but allegations must be backed up with facts, not rumours.

● **Let us reject a culture of 'do nothing so we cannot be blamed if it goes wrong'.** Sometimes people are scared of taking action in case they are blamed. This climate of fear results in a wasting of Army resources and lost opportunities for Kingdom growth. Remember Jesus' teaching about the parable of the talents (Matthew 25:14-30)? We are accountable for what we do not do as much as for what we do.

● **Let us move away from a culture of cynicism and negativity.** Yes, the mission is often hard. As Edward Henry Bickersteth wrote (*SASB* 746 v 3):
> I know how hardly souls are wooed and won;
> My choicest laurels are bedewed with tears.

When we experience failure or disappointment we must resist the temptation to become hardened and bitter. We are a people of hope – not of hopelessness. 'If God is for us, who can be against us?' (Romans 8:31). The Lord is still using the Army in many places. Let us humbly learn from others who are producing fruit. One of the key aims of the Accountability Movement is to encourage a culture of learning across the Army. We have much we can learn from each other if we are willing to listen and adapt.

These are a few examples of the culture that the Accountability Movement is encouraging – and those to be rejected. Let us all pray that this movement will result in deeper, more authentic relationships with God and each other. To reiterate, the aim of this movement is to give more opportunities for people to be renewed by God's Spirit and refocused on God's mission to redeem his world.

Don't wait for someone to tell you how to be a good steward. Pray about it, ask God for guidance and then get on with it. The Holy Spirit is already active around the Army. There are accountability initiatives in many territories such as Pakistan, Canada and Bermuda, the United Kingdom with the Republic of Ireland, and there is an innovative collaboration between Zimbabwe, Zambia, Malawi and Southern Africa working with the Switzerland, Austria and Hungary Territory. In each instance, there is a slightly different way of encouraging change, but they are all moving in the same direction of greater accountability.

Are you ready to commit yourself to being more accountable in your life? Not just for money, property or other physical resources, but also for your relationship with God and your relationships with family, friends, neighbours – not forgetting fellow Salvationists! As *The Salvation Army Handbook of Doctrine* (p 197) explains, we have a high calling: 'To realise Jesus' radical ethic of love is to treat all our relationships as holy covenants. God is able to love through us.' Let us all seek God's will in every part of our lives and be willing to answer tough questions when our relationships fall short of a holy covenant.

Finally ...

Please pray for God's blessing, wisdom and grace to fill this process. It is never easy to change. If the Accountability Movement is only a human creation it will fail. If God is at the heart of the Accountability Movement it will bear much fruit for his Kingdom. Your prayers and active support are essential.

Note: *Journey of Renewal* has been kept as brief as possible to enable translation into many languages. Its contents must be accessible to Salvation Army people around the world. More resources are being developed and will be available to download from **www.salvationarmy.org/accountability**

NOTES

GLOSSARY OF TERMS

The following definitions are drawn from a variety of sources including _The Salvation Army Year Book_ and _The Oxford English Dictionary_.

Accountability Movement: An opportunity for the people and the organisational structures of The Salvation Army to be renewed by God's Spirit and refocused on God's mission to redeem his world.

Activities: The actions of people linked to a Salvation Army programme that are intended to achieve the programme's purpose (e.g. the activities organised for a youth group).

Adherent: An adherent of The Salvation Army is a person who believes in the Lord Jesus Christ and seeks to follow and be like him; participates in the worship, fellowship, service and support of a local Salvation Army congregation; and identifies with the Army's Mission Statement.

Audit: Official examination of management and financial systems, accounts and controls, with verification by reference to witnesses and evidence. There are three types of financial audit in The Salvation Army: (1) internal, (2) external (undertaken by professional, independent auditors) and (3) international (undertaken by IHQ personnel).

Brainstorming: The action or process of making a concerted attempt to solve a problem, usually by a group discussion of spontaneously arising ideas.

Bridgespan Group: A non-profit advisor and resource for mission-driven organisations and philanthropists which collaborates with social sector leaders to help scale impact, build leadership, advance philanthropic effectiveness and accelerate learning. They have worked with The Salvation Army in recent years.

Brief of Appointment (BOA): A document issued to Salvation Army officers outlining their role, responsibilities and outcomes expected in a specific appointment. See also **Memorandum of Appointment**.

Capacity building: The process of developing and strengthening the skills, abilities, processes and resources that organisations and communities need to survive, adapt and thrive in a fast-changing world.

Centre: A Salvation Army social service or community programme located in a building. For example, a hostel for homeless people, a hospital, a school or an older persons care facility.

Chief of the Staff: A Salvation Army officer, appointed by the General, to be second in command of the worldwide Salvation Army.

Chief Secretary: The officer second in command of The Salvation Army in a territory.

Child Protection: The means by which measures are taken and structures put in place to prevent and respond to the abuse of children and ensure children are protected from harm.

Command: A small type of territory.

Corps: A Salvation Army unit established for the preaching of the gospel, worship, teaching and fellowship and to provide Christian-motivated service in the community.

Corps Officer: A Salvation Army officer appointed to a role of spiritual leadership, ministry, administration and pastoral care over a corps.

Covenant: A binding agreement between two parties; in Scripture, the agreement offered to humanity by God of loving faithfulness. The Salvation Army prioritises covenantal relationships. For example: the soldier's covenant, the officer's covenant, the marriage covenant.

Division: A number of corps grouped together under the direction of a divisional commander (may also include social service centres and programmes) operating within a territory or command.

Divisional Commander: The officer in command of the Army in a division.

Divisional leaders: A divisional commander and spouse in their joint role of sharing spiritual leadership and ministry, providing pastoral care and exemplifying the working partnership of officer couples.

Faith-Based Facilitation (FBF): A process that uses specific tools to help people enjoy deeper, healthier relationships. See chapter 10 for more information.

General: The officer elected to the supreme command of the Army throughout the world. All appointments are made, and regulations issued, under the General's authority.

General's Consultative Council (GCC): Established in July 2001, the GCC advises the General on broad matters relating to the Army's mission strategy and policy. Under the chairmanship of the General, selected personnel gather for meetings, not more than three times a year, at a venue determined by the General.

Governance: The framework of rules and practices by which a 'top policy-making group' ensures accountability, fairness and transparency in an organisation's relationship with all of its stakeholders (soldiers, adherents, officers, employees, clients, donors, government, community members). The governance structure includes: (1) the distribution of rights, responsibilities and rewards, (2) procedures for reconciling conflicts of interest and (3) procedures for supervision, control, information flow, and checks and balances.

Impact measurement: A process involving tools used to measure the difference a programme makes on a specific person, group of people or specific location. The definition of impact depends specifically on the goals and the issues being addressed.

Inputs: The raw materials that are used in a Salvation Army programme. These can include money, technical expertise, relationships and personnel.

International Conference of Leaders (ICL): A conference called occasionally by the General of all territorial, command and senior international leaders.

International Headquarters (IHQ): The offices in which the business connected with the administration and supervision of the worldwide Army is transacted.

International Management Council (IMC): The IMC comprises the General and World President of Women's Ministries, the Chief of the Staff and World Secretary for Women's Ministries, all International Secretaries and Zonal Secretaries for Women's Ministries, and the USA National Commander and National President of Women's Ministries. The Council usually meets monthly with the General in the chair.

International Positional Statement: The views expressed in an International Positional Statement constitute the official position of The Salvation Army on the issue addressed. International Positional Statements will be issued when it is possible to state a clear, unequivocal position, with international application, on any social, moral or ethical issue. International Positional Statements may be used in support of public advocacy or action by Salvation Army territories and commands. A positional statement is not binding upon any individual Salvationist with regard to a personal position/opinion on any issue.

Junior soldier: A boy or girl who, having accepted Jesus as their Saviour, has signed the Junior Soldier's Promise and become a Salvationist.

Kairos experience: See chapter 10.

Kingdom of God: The completion of God's purposes for the whole universe can be illustrated in the biblical language of the Kingdom of God. This language is a way of describing the rule of God in human affairs, and is demonstrated when lives and human communities are transformed by Christ. The Bible looks forward to that transformation being made complete and visible in a new world order under God (*Handbook of Doctrine*, pp 224, 230ff).

Leadership development: A structured process to identify, assess, train and educate people to ensure they have the capacity to hold leadership positions in The Salvation Army.

Measurement: The act or process of measuring something. In Salvation Army programmes this can involve measuring activities, outputs, outcomes and impact.

Memorandum of Appointment (MOA): A document issued to senior leaders in The Salvation Army (for example, territorial commanders) outlining their role, responsibilities and outcomes expected in a specific appointment. See also **Brief of Appointment**.

Mission Accountability Framework (MAF): A six-dimension tool to help people be more accountable as they explore what boundless salvation could look like in their lives and for their communities. It helps people plan and track progress towards a common purpose: life in all its fullness as offered by Jesus (John 10:10).

Officer: A Salvationist who has been trained, commissioned and ordained to service and leadership in response to God's call. An officer is a recognised minister of religion.

One Army Accountability and Assessment Review: A review approved by the General in 2013, tasked with producing a written report and set of recommendations for the International Management Council to ensure existing Salvation Army systems meet today's standards. One outcome of the Review was the Accountability Movement.

One Army Impact Initiative: An engagement between IHQ and The Bridgespan Group in coordination with territories around the world to: (1) improve the capacity of The Salvation Army to measure and describe the impact of its activities and (2) encourage a continually evolving learning culture, creating learning communities of practice with a common learning agenda. One outcome of the Initiative was the Accountability Movement work stream focusing on impact measurement.

Orders and Regulations: The orders and regulations of The Salvation Army together make up a manual of operations for furthering the mission on which Salvationists are engaged.

Outcomes: The benefits that a Salvation Army programme is designed to deliver (e.g. the number of young people who become junior soldiers as a result of the Sunday school programme).

GLOSSARY

Outputs: The tangible and intangible products that result from the activities of a Salvation Army programme (e.g. the number of meals served at a disaster site).

Prioritising: Arranging (items) to be dealt with in order of importance; to establish priorities for (a set of items).

Ranks of officers: Lieutenant, Captain, Major, Lieut-Colonel, Colonel, Commissioner, General.

Risk management: The deployment of risk assessment and management tools, and internal controls that increase the likelihood of mission effectiveness and efficiency.

Safeguarding: A total commitment by The Salvation Army to the well-being, safeguarding and protection of all people – particularly children and vulnerable adults such as the elderly and disabled – by implementing best practice in every expression of Salvation Army contact and influence.

Salvation: The mission of God, through Jesus Christ, to redeem the whole world. *The Handbook of Doctrine* (p 152) provides more detail: 'Salvation means we are accepted by God unconditionally and promised a new way of life through him … To be saved is far more than to receive a personal new life: we are part of God's new society, his people called to convey the good news to the world … Furthermore, salvation in the biblical sense does not only concern individuals and communities but affects the entire world order. We are promised "a new Heaven and a new earth".'

Senior soldier: A converted person at least 14 years of age who has, with the approval of the senior pastoral care council, been enrolled as a member of The Salvation Army after signing the Soldier's Covenant.

SMART: Specific, Measurable, Achievable, Realistic and Time-related.

Steward: Being a good steward has a specific meaning for Christians grounded in the New Testament. Paul and the Early Church disciples regarded themselves as stewards of the mysteries of God (1 Corinthians 4:1-2). The idea is that Christians are to take scrupulous care of that which was entrusted to us by God, and give it out to others faithfully and as directed by Jesus Christ. Peter considered himself and all other Christians as 'stewards of the manifold grace of God' (1 Peter 4:10 *KJV*).

Sustainable Development Goals: A set of 17 goals agreed by all 193 member states of the United Nations to be achieved by 2030.

Territorial Commander: The officer in command of the Army in a territory.

Territorial leaders: A territorial commander and spouse in their joint role of sharing spiritual leadership and ministry, providing pastoral care and exemplifying the working partnership of officer couples.

Territory: A country, part of a country or several countries combined, in which Salvation Army work is organised under a territorial commander. Smaller units are known as Commands or Regions, organised under an Officer Commanding or Regional Commander.

United Nations: An international organisation founded in 1945. It is currently made up of 193 member states. The mission and work of the United Nations are guided by the purposes and principles contained in its founding Charter.

Zone(s): A collection of Salvation Army territories, commands and regions in a geographical area. The zonal departments are the main administrative link between IHQ and territories, commands or regions. The international secretaries give oversight to and coordinate the Army's work in their respective geographical areas.